Teacher

Peggy J. Parks

KIDHAVEN PRESS™

THOMSON
GALE

San Diego • Detroit • New York • San Francisco • Cleveland
New Haven, Conn. • Waterville, Maine • London • Munich

LIBRARY OF CONGRESS CATALOGING-IN-PUBLICATION DATA

Parks, Peggy J., 1951–
  Teacher / by Peggy J. Parks.
    v. cm.—(Exploring careers series)
  Includes bibliographical references and index.
  Contents: Different kinds of teachers—What it takes to be a teacher—Life in the classroom—Meet a teacher.
  ISBN 0-7377-1487-5 (hardback : alk. paper)
  1. Teachers—United States—Juvenile literature. 2. Teaching—Vocational guidance—United States—Juvenile literature. [1. Teachers. 2. Occupations.] I. Title. II. Series.
  LB1775.2 .P35 2003
  371-1—dc21

                                   2002014470

CONTENTS

Different Kinds of Teachers

"**I**f you can read this, thank a teacher" is sometimes seen on car bumper stickers. In just a few words, that phrase describes how valuable teachers are. They help children learn about the countries of the world and the stars in the sky, famous people from the past and predictions for the future. They teach math, science, and history, and they help children learn why this information matters in their lives. Because of teachers, children of all ages gain knowledge and a better understanding of the world around them.

Different Varieties

Teachers work in many different types of schools. Most teach in public schools, which vary in size based on where they are located. For instance, the

New York City public school system employs more than 600,000 full-time teachers in its 15,500 elementary, middle, and high schools. In stark contrast to that is Alaska's Northwest Arctic Borough school district, which is one of the most rural and remote school districts in the country. It has just 12 schools and employs 27 teachers.

In addition to public schools, some teachers work in private schools, or **parochial** (religious) **schools**. Others work in **charter schools**, which are a specialized kind of public school. Some teachers work in small schools where children of different ages are taught together in the same classroom. One example of this type of school is on Mackinac Island, a

This biology teacher uses melon heads to add a creative touch to an anatomy lesson.

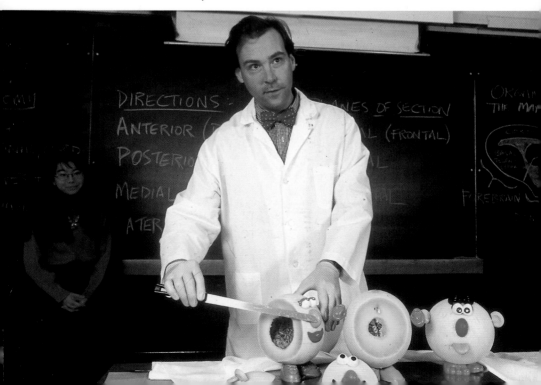

small island off the coast of northern Michigan. Only about six hundred people live there year-round, and fewer than one hundred students from kindergarten through twelfth grade attend Mackinac Island School. The classes are very small, with only about six students in each class. Plus, something else is unusual about this school besides its small size. Mackinac Island does not allow any cars, so teachers and students must ride bikes or walk to school when the weather is nice. In the winter months, a horse-drawn carriage serves as a "school bus."

Preschool and Kindergarten Teachers

Some teachers work with very young children. Those who teach preschool work with children who are three or four years old and may be away from home for the first time. Preschool teachers understand that this can be a frightening experience, so they spend time helping children get over their fears. They help students learn how to get along with others, how to share, and how to participate in classroom activities. Basically, preschool teachers prepare children for what to expect when they go to school like the "big kids."

Kindergarten teachers are similar to preschool teachers because they work with young children. Some of these children have attended preschool, so they have learned what it is like to spend time in a classroom. For others, kindergarten is their first real

These preschool students learn sharing and class participation by playing games with their teacher.

experience with school. That means teachers must be prepared to work with children who have different levels of knowledge and social skills. Those who are shy or afraid require more of a teacher's time, until they become comfortable around other children.

Kindergarten teacher Elaine Kuegler says that her biggest challenge is to help her students excel in tasks they feel they cannot do, as well as the tasks they enjoy. Also, she finds it challenging to keep the advanced students busy and interested while she helps others learn basic math and reading skills. In spite of the challenges, Kuegler enjoys her job, and says she likes the unpredictable nature of teaching young children: "I never quite know ahead of time what will happen when these kindergarten children walk into my classroom. Every day presents new challenges and also wonderful rewards."[1]

Elementary School Teachers

Teachers who work in elementary schools teach students in first through fifth or sixth grade. They usually work with one grade at a time, in one classroom, and they have the same students for the whole school year. Elementary teachers educate their students about many different subjects, including English, reading, math, social studies, and science. Some teachers teach in multilevel classrooms, which means they have students who are at different levels in their learning. For instance, some students might be average learners, while others work at a higher level and faster pace than their classmates.

Instead of teaching many different subjects, elementary teachers may specialize in one subject, such as art, reading, or music. These teachers travel between different classrooms in the same school, or they might travel from school to school. Roberta Guaspara-Tzavaras is a violin teacher who works with young children in East Harlem, one of New York City's poorest neighborhoods. She believes that all children should have the opportunity to learn music because of the joy and discipline it brings to their lives. One student began studying violin when she was in the first grade. By the time she was twelve years old, she had performed in Switzerland, and she had also played for Oprah Winfrey.

This elementary school teacher dresses as the cartoon character Arthur to engage his students.

A music teacher prepares her students for a violin recital.

Secondary School Teachers

Teachers who work in middle schools or high schools are often called **secondary school** teachers. They usually specialize in one or two subjects. In most secondary schools, students travel to different rooms for each of their classes. For example, a middle school science teacher or a high school algebra teacher would usually teach six or seven classes each day to separate groups of students.

Middle school teachers face some unique challenges in their jobs because of the ages of their students. Susan Ray has been teaching middle school for ten years, and she says that many teachers do not want to teach this age group. For her, the key to being successful with middle schoolers is to let them know that she believes they can succeed. She also makes it clear to them that she understands what they are going through, as she explains: "You see, I remember what it was like to be a seventh grader. I remember going to school and realizing that what I thought was going to be the 'in' fashion was really the 'out' fashion. I remember having a pimple on my nose the size of Cleveland and knowing that everyone noticed it too. I remember coming home and crying because I realized that I wasn't accepted in the most popular crowd . . . I tell them that I am going to believe in each one of them until they can begin to believe in themselves."[2]

Special Education Teachers

Some teachers work with students who have special needs. These could include physical or emotional disabilities, or **cognitive disabilities**, such as lower-than-average intelligence. Denver special education teacher Julie Spilsted says that her job can be frustrating at times, but for the most part it is highly rewarding. "A teacher is someone who teaches because it is a passion. I would say I'm part teacher, part psychologist, part social worker, and part cheerleader. I never

This special education teacher instructs students at a school for deaf children by helping them form words with their hands.

A biology teacher carefully handles a Royal Python.
Teachers must be dedicated to helping their students learn.

forget that something I do might make a positive difference in a child's life. There is no greater reward than that."[3]

Whether they teach kindergarten or high school, ABCs or astrophysics, teachers are extremely important. They are people whose careers are devoted to one goal: making a difference in their students' lives by helping them learn.

CHAPTER 2

What It Takes to Be a Teacher

There are certain personal qualities that all teachers need. For example, teachers must enjoy being surrounded by young people. They must genuinely care about their students, and have the desire and willingness to help them learn. They must be enthusiastic about teaching, so they can lead and inspire. They must be understanding, and perhaps most important of all, must be patient. In fact, most teachers agree that the most important quality is an above-average supply of patience.

Teachers must also be able to relate well with all kinds of students. Children come from many different **ethnic** backgrounds, religions, and races. They also come from different economic circumstances—some have very poor families, while others have wealthy families. Teachers must treat all students fairly and equally, and not be prejudiced or biased in favor of one particular group.

Learning to Teach

Teachers need different kinds of education and training based on where they teach, what subjects they teach, and the ages of their students. All teachers must attend a four-year college and earn a bachelor's degree. The courses they take often vary based on the college. In most cases college courses are related to what aspiring teachers plan to teach. For instance, someone who wants to teach biology must earn a certain number of college credits in biology, as well as in other science courses. Someone who plans to

A biology teacher helps a group of elementary school kids get acquainted with a small shark.

teach elementary school must learn about a variety of different subjects, as well as take classes that focus on elementary education. Special education teachers need to take courses in psychology, sociology, and specialized subjects that deal with different types of disabilities.

College students who plan to become teachers are assigned student teaching jobs, usually during their last year of college. This is their first opportunity to apply what they have learned to the real

One-on-one instruction is an important part of building personal relationships with students.

world of teaching. The assignment usually lasts for a semester, and student teachers are supervised by senior-level teachers who act as their mentors and coaches.

Once students earn their college degree and finish their student teaching assignments, they must complete another step before they become teachers. All states require teachers to be certified. They achieve certification by completing the required college program, and by passing a state certification examination.

Even after people become certified teachers, their education does not end. Most states require teachers to keep their knowledge current by continuing their education through workshops and classes. Also, teachers usually have to retake tests every few years to keep their certifications current. Some states, such as New York, allow teachers to become permanently certified. To do this, they must earn advanced degrees, such as a master's or doctorate (Ph.D.), work in teaching positions for several years, and pass a special examination.

Building Relationships

Teachers learn a lot of valuable information while they are in college. However, they learn most of what they need to know by actually teaching. One of the first lessons teachers learn is the importance of building good relationships with students. No two students are alike, and the best teachers are those who get to know their students personally. Fourth-grade teacher Mary Cotterall says that building relationships with students is important if teachers want to do their jobs well. She says that when children misbehave in class, or get bad grades, it may be because something is troubling them. Perhaps they have problems at home, or did not have breakfast before going to school. She explains: "Children suffer from stress too. I had one little girl who was terribly upset because it was her birthday, and neither of her parents remembered to send a birthday treat to school. I've had other students who recently lost a favorite pet. Things like that are difficult for children, and it can affect their ability to learn."[4]

Personal relationships between teachers and students are important for older students, too. High school teacher Darci J. Harland chose education as her career because she wanted to make a difference in the lives of teenagers. She discusses her perspective on building relationships: "The first year . . . I did not have time or the energy to really get to know my students. The second year, however, I was able to reach out a bit more. This is [so] rewarding! It means so much to me when students confide in me, or just tell me about themselves outside my classroom."[5]

Dealing with Problems

All teachers wish they never had behavior problems with their students. However, students do sometimes get into trouble and teachers must be prepared

This teacher explains answers from a biology test, helping students better understand the subject matter.

to deal with them. Discipline and order are extremely important, and good teachers know that students must respect them as authority figures. Harland says that all students benefit from discipline, and all students want it—even if they may not know it. "We know that the 'good' student who wants to learn appreciates a disciplined classroom, but even the trouble-causers and attention-seekers like discipline. They all may not admit this to you, but there is a satisfaction in knowing the standards that are set in a classroom day after day are constant."[6] Harland also says that once teachers give up control to students, it is impossible for them to get that control back.

The Teacher as Coach

Teachers deal with different challenges based on the ages of their students. However, no matter how young or how old their students are, teachers must be able to motivate them. The more motivated students are, the more they will want to learn. This can be challenging for teachers, because students often do not understand why they need to learn certain subjects. So, teachers must try to create interest and excitement in subjects that students may not normally find interesting.

Sometimes teachers motivate students by encouraging them to participate in extracurricular activities. Eddie Wexler, a history teacher and **debate** coach in Richmond, California, formed a debate team at the school where he teaches. The school's area is extremely poor, and it is located in a high-crime area. Many students are not interested in learning and do not do their work. However, those who are involved in debate have dramatically improved their grades. Some have become straight-A students. Also, they have become more motivated to learn and have better attitudes about school. Students who once considered dropping out of school are now determined to graduate from college. Wexler believes that debate has transformed

A science teacher helps a student with an experiment.

After-school activities, such as this music class, often motivate students to do well in school.

his students' lives: "Debate has helped my kids find their voices. And now, in a society that has pretty much ignored them, they will have a greatly improved ability to make themselves heard."[7]

Most teachers say that to do their jobs well, they must be more than teachers. They must also be psychologists, coaches, mind readers, and drill sergeants. Teaching school is not an easy job, and sometimes it can be difficult. However, there are many talented, dedicated teachers who believe it is the best job in the world.

CHAPTER 3

Life in the Classroom

The tasks that teachers perform vary based on their individual jobs. They do have some things in common, such as being on their feet a lot during the day, teaching lessons, and giving tests. Also, most teachers work many hours outside the classroom. Their "official" workday may end after the last school bell rings, but they often prepare tests, grade daily assignments, and grade tests while they are away from school.

In addition to teaching in the classroom, most teachers keep regular office hours so students may seek their help outside of class. This may involve helping students who are having problems in the class, or providing extra instruction for those who are falling behind. In addition, teachers hold parent-teacher conferences several times a year. This gives them an opportunity to talk with parents about the students' progress.

Most teachers work from late August through June. Some also teach summer school, and others work at a different job, or take the summer off. Many teachers spend at least part of their summer attending workshops or taking classes, to learn how to be better teachers.

Teaching Through Play

Teachers who work with preschoolers know that these children learn mainly through play activities. To teach language skills, they use such activities as

Preschoolers learn through a variety of playful activities such as this interactive listening game.

storytelling and acting games. To teach the importance of getting along with others, teachers might encourage children to work together to build a neighborhood in a sandbox. To introduce math concepts, they could show children how to balance and count blocks when building a bridge. To teach science concepts, they might show children how to make different paint designs by mixing colors together. Teachers also use creative activities such as art, dance, and music. In most preschool classes, each day's activities include a mix of individual and group play, quiet time, and active time in groups.

Like preschool teachers, kindergarten teachers sometimes use play techniques with their students. According to Kuegler, kindergartners are often at different levels—some are very advanced, and others cannot even count to ten. In her class, she teaches letters and sounds, works on simple math problems, and begins teaching students how to read. She says the hardest part of her job is keeping all of the children involved. Plus, she must spend extra time with children who need more help. She says when these children finally grasp the concepts they had found so difficult, she is overjoyed.

Working with Elementary Students

As students move up into higher grades, elementary school teachers help them expand their knowledge. They teach students to be better readers, and they teach them math problems such as multiplication and division. They also teach students about history, science, English, and geography.

Teachers in an Atlanta, Georgia, elementary school use a creative method of teaching their students. They use puppets. The children make their own puppets and write scripts for puppet shows, which are based on subjects such as social studies, literature, and science. One teacher says that by using puppets, the students learn to understand, not just memorize, information: "It gives the kids a chance to get inside a story and feel what they're hearing and seeing, rather than letting it just wash over them as a bunch of facts."[8]

Being a Creative Teacher

Mary Cotterall says the best method teachers can use is to teach students how what they learn relates to the real world. For instance, when students want to know why they need to learn math, she tells them this: "If I have a birthday party and one hundred people are coming, I may want to serve cupcakes. Some of the guests may eat two cupcakes, and some may eat three cupcakes, so I need math to figure out how many to make." She also teaches her students by involving them in creative projects. For instance, to teach Michigan history, she coaches her students in a musical play. For two months they rehearse their lines and their songs, and then they perform the musical at the end of each school year.

Cotterall says the play has worked very well, and it has taught her students a lot about history: "In fact, when they go into fifth grade and study American history, they sometimes break out in the songs they learned when they were in the musical!"[9]

A middle school student plays the Statue of Liberty in a historical musical.

Teaching Teenagers

Many secondary school teachers share Cotterall's philosophy about relating what students learn to the real world. Daniel Robb, a teacher in Massachusetts, is one of them. Robb wanted his advanced geology students to understand how the ice age has shaped the landscape. So, each day he and the students went outside the classroom and walked around the town. Together they observed the beaches, hills, swamps, valleys, and rocks, and they discussed how these land formations had developed over time. In the classroom, they talked about what they had seen. They also built models of miniature glaciers, and discussed how sediment moves through bodies of water. By the end of the class, the students had seen for themselves how the land where they lived had been formed. They also understood why geology was important. Robb tells of a conversation between one student and his father, as they walked along the beach. The boy pointed at a large boulder and said, "See Dad that's granite, and it had time to cool, so its crystals are all lumpy. But if it had cooled quick, then it would be all smooth, so we could make a knife of it."[10] After hearing this, Robb knew he had done more than just teach students about rocks. He also helped shape their interest in why nature had caused the rocks to be there in the first place.

Sometimes secondary school teachers work in unusual places—such as a farm. Teachers at Walter

A junior high art teacher shows students how to spin pottery.

B. Saul High School in Philadelphia work at the school's one-hundred-acre farm, which is located across the street. The farm has cows, two kinds of sheep, a llama, horses, pigs, and chickens. Saul teachers help prepare students for careers in agriculture, horticulture, or veterinary medicine. One teacher, Dave Snyder, says that the farm teaches students about much more than just how to care for animals, or how to raise crops. It also helps them get over their fears of trying new things, taking risks, and getting dirty. He believes these are important for students to learn, as he explains: "Those are life skills that make a student successful no matter what their future."[11]

Teaching Special Needs Students

Special education teachers work with students who have many different disabilities. This means their specific teaching methods will vary based on the students' individual needs. Spilsted typically works with children in small groups. If she is teaching them reading and writing skills, she might spend an entire class working on word sounds. She explains: "One day we might work on the long sound of the letter 'U.' We first talk about the sound, and then maybe we'll use magnetic letters to make words with the letter. Then we'll read a story that has a lot of words with long 'U' sounds, and follow that with a writing exercise."[12] Spilsted uses the same basic practice to teach math

A boy requiring special attention gets a boost from a special education teacher.

concepts. She describes a math problem to her students, and then she uses objects such as blocks or pennies to illustrate it for them.

Teachers may teach in a classroom, or they may teach on a farm. They may teach students to use e-mail, or how to hand-write letters using cursive. They may teach little tots in preschool or seniors in high school. Yet no matter what subjects or classes they teach, all teachers measure their own success by the success of their students.

CHAPTER 4

Meet a Teacher

Jeff Reeths is a fourth grade teacher at North Muskegon Elementary School in Muskegon, Michigan. He has been an elementary school teacher for six years. Reeths says that one reason he decided to teach school was because of his family. His mother was an elementary school teacher for forty-two years, and his four siblings are all teachers. However, the biggest reason he chose a teaching career was because of how much he enjoyed being around children.

Before I became a teacher, I worked in broadcasting and had a background in drama and theater. I loved teaching theater classes to children during the summer and on weekends. They energized me, and I found that they taught me as much as I taught them. I also discovered that children have so much enthusiasm and imagination—two qualities that are often lacking in adults. Since I enjoyed working with them so much, I decided to do it for a living. I've never been sorry.[13]

What Makes a Good Teacher

Reeths says there was a time when he thought the most important quality for teachers was complete mastery of the subjects they taught. He now realizes that other qualities are more important.

> I've learned that what really matters are the human qualities—things like a passion for teaching, a sense of humor, the ability to laugh at ourselves. Laughing at myself definitely came in handy during my first year of teaching. I took my students on a nature hike, and I made the mistake of giving the compass to a nine-year-old. About 45

This teacher helps her students learn the geography of the United States.

minutes later, when we were still wandering around the sand dunes without any idea of where we were, I finally took control of the compass. We started back, and were met by a search party of parents and teachers. For three weeks after that, people left maps to the staff lounge on my door, parents brought me Cub Scout books so I could learn basic trail skills, and everyone gave me a hard time. They simply would not let me forget it. Good thing I could laugh at myself!

Teachers also need the ability to understand students, and to personally connect with them. No two children are alike. They all have very different needs, and they all learn at their own pace. You can never give up on them. I had a little girl in one of my classes who struggled in math all year long. We spent many hours after school counting M&Ms and pretzels and exploring every possible way to help her grasp math concepts. On the last day of school, all the other children were outside for recess and she stayed in the room. She told me she didn't want to go outside because she "wanted to stay in fourth grade just a little longer." As teachers, we need to remember that there's a student like that in every classroom. I keep a little sign on my desk that says "Students will not care what you know until they know how much you care." There is so much truth to that.

A Typical Day

Reeths says he normally likes to arrive at school an hour earlier than his students, to prepare for the day.

A middle school teacher uses a word game to help her student learn to spell.

He sets up his room, puts assignments on the board, and checks to be sure he has all his classroom materials ready. After the students arrive, he takes attendance and their lessons begin.

We normally start each day with spelling. On Mondays we review the week's words, and on Fridays we have spelling tests. After spelling we work on reading for about an hour. We'll discuss a particular story, and talk about different reading methods. We spend quite a bit of time on reading because it is such an important skill, and I really want them to enjoy it. After that we work on English, writing, history, math, and other subjects.

Reeths says that no matter what he teaches, he wants his students to do more than just learn about a subject. He wants them to understand *why* they are learning about subjects. "When I was young, I found myself wondering 'why do I need to know this?' I don't want my students to ask that—I want them to know that everything they learn connects in some way with real life."

An elementary school teacher explains to a student the importance of developing strong writing skills.

Why He Teaches

Sometimes people who are not teachers ask Reeths why he teaches.

> I answer by saying that I teach because it's my passion. I love it. I feel like I'm making a positive difference in the lives of young people. I've always said that if I ever find myself walking into a classroom and dreading the day ahead, then it would be time to quit. That hasn't happened. I can come in here half asleep and grumpy, yet as soon as my kids get in the room, they brighten the day.
>
> Of course teaching has its challenging points, just like any job. I'm fortunate to work in a good school district where there really aren't many problems. However, some teachers aren't so lucky. Those who teach in the poorer schools have kids who bring a lot of baggage to school with them. In fact, their teacher may be the only stable adult they know. I've known teachers who spent their time off at Wal-Mart buying hats and mittens for students who didn't have any. These situations are very sad, yet the teachers still have a chance to make a difference in the lives of their students.

Heartwarming Experience

Reeths has had many memorable experiences in his six years of teaching, but one in particular stands out. It involved the same little girl who had not wanted to leave his fourth grade class. She had finished elementary school and was ready to enter junior high. Her mother wrote Reeths a letter and told

In an attempt to motivate her students, this elementary school music teacher donates her hair to a charity group.

him she had asked her daughter what she would miss most about elementary school. The girl's reply was, "Pizza Hut Pizza Day and Mr. Reeths." The mother also wrote that the extra time Reeths had spent with her daughter made a huge difference—that he made her believe she was capable, and that she could succeed. "That's a perfect example of what can happen when a teacher really cares. When a child wants to learn, you don't mind the extra effort, you just do whatever you need to do. In the end, the experience you give them is the experience that's going to stay with them for a long time."

Message for Kids

Reeths says that anyone considering a career in teaching needs to be enthusiastic about it, and motivated to spend their days helping young people.

> A lot of kids want to become teachers because they know they'll have summers off, or because their students will give them presents. However, if you're going to be a good teacher, you need enthusiasm for the job. Think about the teachers you've really liked, the ones who made learning fun. They were interesting and funny, they did special things in class, they valued what you had to say. That's important. That's the difference between being a good teacher, and being a great teacher.

N O T E S

Chapter 1: Different Kinds of Teachers

1. Elaine Kuegler, "A Day in the Life of an Elementary School Teacher." www.skyline.net.

2. Susan Ray, "Teaching Middle Level Kids: Remember Seventh Grade?" *In Case You Missed It* section of *Middleweb*. www.middleweb.com.

3. Julie Spilsted, interview by author, July 19, 2002.

Chapter 2: What It Takes to Be a Teacher

4. Mary Cotterall, interview by author, July 18, 2002.

5. Darci J. Harland, "Discipline as a New Teacher." www.iloveteaching.com.

6. Harland, "Discipline as a New Teacher."

7. Quoted in David Ruenzel, "Making Themselves Heard," *Teacher Magazine,* April 2002.

Chapter 3: Life in the Classroom

8. Quoted in Candice Dyer, "Helping Hands," *Teacher Magazine,* May 2002.

9. Cotterall, interview.

10. Quoted in Daniel Robb, "No Stone Unturned," *Teacher Magazine,* April 2002.

11. Quoted in Debra Gordon, "Farm Team," *Teacher Magazine,* November 2001.

12. Spilsted, interview.

Chapter 4: Meet a Teacher

13. All quotes in Chapter 4: Jeff Reeths, interview by author, August 28, 2002.

GLOSSARY

charter school: A public school that is free from many local and state regulations in exchange for agreeing to meet certain student performance standards.

cognitive disabilities: Difficulties in learning caused by a person's mental capacity, which affects the ability to think, reason, or remember.

debate: A formal discussion with arguments for and against a particular topic.

ethnic: Relates to a group of people who have common national, cultural, or tribal origins.

parochial school: A school connected with a religious institution.

secondary school: A term used to describe middle school, junior high school, or high school.

FOR FURTHER EXPLORATION

Books

Carol Kelly-Gangi, *Celebrating Teachers.* New York: Barnes & Noble, 2001. A collection of observations by teachers and students.

Jim Murphy, *My Face to the Wind.* New York: Scholastic, 2001. The true story of Sarah Jane Price, a teenage girl who writes about her experiences as a teacher in Nebraska during the late 1800s.

David Shribman, *I Remember My Teacher,* Kansas City, MO: Andrews McMeel, 2001. A collection of personal stories about teachers and the effect they have had on their students' lives.

Esther Wright, *Why I Teach.* Roseville, CA: Prima, 1999. An inspiring collection of stories written by teachers who love the challenges and triumphs of teaching.

Jim Yerman, *So You Want to Be a Special Education Teacher.* Arlington, TX: Future Horizons, 2001. A book about the challenges and successes experienced by a teacher who works with students who have special needs.

Internet Sources

SoYouWanna.com, "So You Wanna Be a Teacher?" www.soyouwanna.com.

U.S. Department of Labor, Bureau of Labor Statistics *Occupational Outlook Handbook* 2002–2003, "Teachers—

Preschool, Kindergarten, Elementary, Middle, and Secondary," www.bls.gov.

Websites

LessonPlansPage.com (www.lessonplanspage.com). Includes a collection of links to stories for and about teachers.

Teacher Magazine (www.teachermagazine.org). An online magazine with essays, articles, and commentaries written by teachers.

INDEX

PICTURE CREDITS

Peggy J. Parks holds a Bachelor of Science degree from Aquinas College in Grand Rapids, Michigan, where she graduated magna cum laude. She is a freelance writer who has written a number of books for The Gale Group, including the KidHaven Press Exploring Careers series, the Lucent Books Careers for the 21st Century series, and the Blackbirch Press Giants of Science and Nations in Crisis series. Parks was also the profile writer for the Towery Publications book, *Grand Rapids: The City That Works.* She lives in Muskegon, Michigan, a town that she says inspires her writing because of its location on the shores of Lake Michigan.